# The Estate Settler's Organizer

## FOR SETTLING AN UNMARRIED FRIEND OR FAMILY MEMBER'S ESTATE

Teresa M. O'Brien

# The Estate Settler's Organizer

## For Settling an Unmarried
## Friend or Family Member's Estate

Disclaimer: While helpful hints and reminders are provided throughout the book for completing the tables, they are in no way to be considered a substitute for legal and financial counsel. Please check with all the members of your professional team for the latest requirements and processes. O'Brien Consulting Group, LLC., assumes no responsibility for legal or financial processes.

# Table of Contents

# INTRODUCTION

I wrote this book for those of you like myself, who are responsible for settling your last living parent's estate. It can also be used as a guide for settling any unmarried person's estate and also as a "conversation starter guide" for pre-planning.

This workbook is a combination of the learnings my sister and I developed as we handled our responsibilities as executors and trustees (she for her husband's estate and me for our mother's estate). The tables in this book can be used with the advice you are following from any book or professional.

There are many excellent executor and trustee books – some of which are listed at the end of this book – on what must be done, through whom, and caveats on the process. But the actual tables to help you organize your information are usually left up to you to create. This book is designed to fill that gap.

My sister and I found that often closing an account could be a multi-step process. Something that you could do in ten minutes on your own account could take hours and days to complete for an estate. Part of the reason that you will likely have to talk with multiple people to close an estate account is that only certain people in an organization are authorized to handle these account closures. Getting to these people in an organization can require talking to more than one individual.

So being able to track where you are in the process with each account is important. This is especially true when working with multiple organizations simultaneously.

# HOW TO USE THIS WORKBOOK

The process of settling an estate can take months, and in some cases years, to complete. This book provides an organized way to note your progress while addressing the necessary steps to settling the estate. Write on the pages, add sticky notes, highlight lines – whatever you find helpful.

This book helps you track what is completed and what is still in progress. For those items that are incomplete, you can note what actions are being taken and by whom. When everything is done, keep the book as a reminder of how accounts were handled.

**NOTE: <u>Keep copies of everything that you send by US Postal Mail. Copy yourself on every email that you send.</u>** Not only will this help you remember what you have sent, but if the recipient fails to get your message, you can quickly resend the information. It also makes it easy to jointly discuss any follow-up over the phone.

You may often find that you start each contact with a new company by leaving messages. Therefore, spend a few minutes writing down bullet points for why you are calling so you can leave a short message. Always give your name, your deceased's legal name, and your call back number twice in the call – once at the beginning and once at the end. Having all that information at the very beginning of the call makes it easier for them to re-listen to the call for any of it that they missed. Having it at the end gives them a second chance to get all of it the first time through the message. When you do reach someone, always ask for a direct line number for any further callbacks or in case you get disconnected.

Be patient with yourself and others but be persistent. Get a commitment for a date when any required action will likely be completed and get a call back number for follow-up when that date arrives. Always get the name of the person you are speaking with. People tend to take a little extra care when they know you care enough about them to find out something as simple as their name.

# FUNERAL PREPARATIONS

If you are responsible for funeral planning, these next few pages can be a helpful resource.

Some funeral homes will coordinate the initial purchase of death certificates. **Funeral homes are the most efficient way to get death certificates if they offer that service in your area. They may even issue a temporary one for you.** Although everyone's situation is different, 10-15 copies should be sufficient since many places will return the original certificate after they have made a copy for their files (especially if accounts are local). Some businesses will accept receipt of death certificates via fax or email.

Most funeral homes will notify Social Security and Veterans Affairs of your deceased one's death, but it pays to follow up to verify notification has taken place. Notifying these agencies as soon as possible is important because only a check that was issued in the month the person was alive can be retained by the estate. Any funds that were received after that time will have to be returned to the agencies.

# FUNERAL ARRANGEMENTS

Funeral homes will talk you through the funeral arrangements, but it is good to take notes and write down any agreements or follow-up questions. Some funeral homes will give you support resources when you use their services. Sort through these resources to find any that will help you and begin using them immediately. If the deceased had previously discussed his/her funeral wishes, bring those to the meeting with the funeral director. Life insurance or pre-paid funeral/burial policies may cover some or all of these expenses.

| Item | Notes |
|---|---|
| **Deceased's written instructions for funeral arrangements** | |
| **Funeral/burial budget** | |
| **Funeral home's pricing options** | |
| **Funeral home's payment terms** | |
| **Items to be buried with deceased** | |
| **Visitation hours** | |
| **Funeral service hours** | |
| **Interment/Inurnment hours** | |
| **Funeral home hours for drop off/pick up of items** | |
| **Burial plot deed** | |

| Item | Notes |
|---|---|
| **Cremation** | |
| **Memorial service** <br> **Funeral observances** <br> **Pallbearers** <br> **Eulogies** <br> **Music** | |
| **Disposition of ashes** | |
| **Transportation** | |
| **Post funeral gathering** | |
| **Food** | |
| **Obituary** | |
| **Flowers** | |
| **Charities for donations** | |
| **Prepaid thank you cards** | |
| **Social Security and VA notifications** | |
| **Death certificates (10-15 certified copies)** | |
| **Prepaid funeral/burial policy** | |

# PAYING FOR THE FUNERAL

Typical sources of readily available funds to pay for the funeral are **pre-paid funeral/burial policies, cash, checking accounts, money market accounts, savings accounts, CDs, credit cards, and brokerage accounts**. Focus here first if your funeral home requires up-front payment for their services (which many funeral homes do).

You will be looking for **accounts that a living person has access to.** If only the deceased had access to the account, the funds in that account could be frozen. Those funds will be released to the estate or trust only after you have presented to the institution both a certified death certificate and papers certifying you as the authorized executor of the estate or trustee of the trust, depending on how the ownership of the account is stated. That can take time to achieve and likely will not be completed until after the funeral.

After meeting with the funeral director, your immediate cash requirement for funeral expenses is $_____. List where the funds can potentially come from on the next page.

# SOURCES OF MONEY TO PAY FOR THE FUNERAL

| Source | Account Number | Available Money | Online UserID | Online Password | Who Has Authorized Access? |
|--------|----------------|-----------------|---------------|-----------------|----------------------------|
|        |                |                 |               |                 |                            |
|        |                |                 |               |                 |                            |
|        |                |                 |               |                 |                            |
|        |                |                 |               |                 |                            |
|        |                |                 |               |                 |                            |
|        |                |                 |               |                 |                            |
|        |                |                 |               |                 |                            |
|        |                |                 |               |                 |                            |
|        |                |                 |               |                 |                            |
|        |                |                 |               |                 |                            |
|        |                |                 |               |                 |                            |

# HELP FROM FAMILY AND FRIENDS

Delegate as many non-financial tasks to others (family, friends, and business colleagues) as possible – especially at the beginning – so that you can stay focused on those things that only YOU must do. Some typical activities are listed below. Add whatever is needed for your situation.

| Activity | Person Responsible | Contact Information | Responsibility Assigned |
|---|---|---|---|
| **Updating family (keep a list with contact info)** | | | |
| **Updating friends (keep a list with contact info)** | | | |
| **Updating co-workers (ask someone from work)** | | | |
| **Watching minor children or special needs dependents** | | | |
| **Cancelling deceased's appointments** | | | |
| **Watching pets** | | | |
| | | | |
| | | | |

# GETTING STARTED

The first thing after the funeral that you will need to address is obtaining the legal papers certifying that you are the trustee of the trust or the executor for the estate. Only then can you begin the process of notifying creditors, paying outstanding bills in priority order, closing accounts, and distributing funds to settle the estate.

It can take weeks to get the legal document from your state or county indicating that you are entitled to represent the interest of the estate. Once you have obtained those official documents, you will have several organizations that you may have to contact multiple times as you begin the process of settling that estate. The next two pages contain tables for you to summarize their contact information or you can put the information into your smartphone.

# KEY DAILY CONTACTS

List the contact information for people and organizations you will likely be contacting multiple times on this page and the next one or put the information into your smartphone.

| Type | Contact Name | Phone | Email | Fax |
|---|---|---|---|---|
| **Funeral home** | | | | |
| **Cemetery** | | | | |
| **Social Security** | | | | |
| **Deceased's current employer** | | | | |
| **Deceased's former employer 1** | | | | |
| **Deceased's former employer 2** | | | | |
| **Medicare** | | | | |
| **Medicaid** | | | | |
| **Veterans Affairs** | | | | |

# PROFESSIONAL TEAM MEMBERS

| Type | Contact Name | Phone | Email | Fax |
|---|---|---|---|---|
| Family lawyer | | | | |
| Business lawyer | | | | |
| Accountant | | | | |
| Financial planner | | | | |
| Insurance representative | | | | |
| | | | | |
| | | | | |

# DISCUSSION WITH AN ATTORNEY: EXECUTING WILL OR TRUST DIRECTIVES

The trust and will documents indicate who will be the trustee of the deceased's trust and the executor of the deceased's estate, respectively. If you are the named individual, verify your acceptance of the responsibilities. If you are the executor of the estate, you will usually have to obtain a document issued by the county or state certifying that you are the legal representative. Institutions will often ask to see this document to verify they can do business with you on behalf of the estate. Since it can take weeks to get this document, this is one of the things you will want to start as soon as possible.

Review the will and trust documents as soon as possible, in case there is anything that needs immediate attention. Prioritize the rest and complete in a timely manner.

Because every state has different legal requirements, it is best to consult with your attorney for guidance about any questions pertaining to these legal documents, such as:

- Will or trust execution process (including certified letters of appointment for personal representative or Letters of Testamentary)
- Filing of will in probate court (if needed)
- Notification of creditors
- Estate's liability for deceased's debts and priority order of claims
- Preparing list of deceased's assets – both non-financial assets (i.e. jewelry, boats, etc.) and financial assets - along with their value at the time of decedent's death
- Handling transition of deceased's business ownership (if applicable)
- Annual estate accounting procedure/paperwork until the estate is closed
- Whom at the law office to contact when you have follow-up questions and that person's contact information
- Attorney's fees for services

# DISCUSSION WITH AN ACCOUNTANT:
## TAXES AND COST BASIS

Some initial topics to cover with your accountant:

- Information accountant needs from you to determine which taxes need filing (both at state and federal level) and by what date
- Required Employer Identification Number (EIN)
- Knowledge of rules of transfer of funds from retirement accounts (IRAs, 401K, 403B, SEPs, SIMPLEs, etc.)
- How to determine the cost basis of the various assets
- Setting up bank accounts in the name of trust or estate to facilitate activities to close the estate
- What records to keep and for how long
- Whom to contact at accountant's office for any follow-up questions and that person's contact information
- Accountant's fees for services

# GATHERING DOCUMENTS

As you settle the estate, there are documents that you will need to take with you to almost every meeting or have available for every phone call. They are listed in the first table below. The second table lists items that may be needed, depending upon the specific meeting. **It is good to collect them all in one convenient location**. Check off each item as you find it. For items, you don't put into this one place, note the item's current location next to the item in the table below. Reminder: Death Certificates can be applied for through the funeral home that handled the deceased's funeral services if your area allows it.

## MOST OFTEN NEEDED DOCUMENTS

| | | | |
|---|---|---|---|
| ☐ | Will | ☐ | Death certificates |
| ☐ | Trust document | ☐ | Military discharge papers |
| ☐ | Deceased's birth certificate | ☐ | Passport or citizenship papers |
| ☐ | Adoption papers | ☐ | Birth certificates of minor children |
| ☐ | Deceased's Social Security card | ☐ | Naturalization papers |
| ☐ | Divorce agreement/decree | ☐ | List of deceased's usernames & passwords |

## DOCUMENTS YOU MAY ALSO NEED

| | | | | | |
|---|---|---|---|---|---|
| ☐ | Life insurance policy numbers | ☐ | Rental property leases | ☐ | Safe-deposit box number and key |
| ☐ | Deceased's employee/retiree number(s) | ☐ | Deeds | ☐ | Storage locker contract and key |
| ☐ | Deceased's Medicare number | ☐ | Loan statements (recent) | ☐ | Annuity contract numbers |
| ☐ | Tax returns (last 2 years) | ☐ | Motor vehicle titles | ☐ | Employee benefits information |
| ☐ | Bank statements (recent) | ☐ | Car insurance | ☐ | Military service records |
| ☐ | Mortgage statements (recent) | ☐ | Homeowner's insurance | ☐ | Record of assets |
| ☐ | Investment account statements (recent) | ☐ | Health insurance | ☐ | Business ownership/interest documents |
| ☐ | Post Office box agreement & key | ☐ | Car lease agreement | ☐ | Postnuptial agreement |
| ☐ | Credit card list | ☐ | Voter registration card | ☐ | Airline mileage numbers |
| ☐ | Prepaid funeral/burial | ☐ | *IRS Form 709 (DSUE) | ☐ | *Transferred lifetime gifts |

*These documents track gift transfers over $15,000 per year/per person & spousal fund transfers at death.

# DOCUMENT TRAVEL BAG

Get a visually distinctive cloth bag or portfolio that can contain:

- all the relevant items in the "Most Often Needed Documents" list on the previous page

- notebook to keep track of tasks and other notes or a 3-ring binder

- pens, paper, binder clips, a Post It© notepad, and a highlighter

- a "reminder" calendar for key dates & follow-up, an easy-to-use calculator

- any meeting-specific paperwork or any paperwork given to you at each meeting

- this book – it was made to be marked up – feel free

**Always put this document travel bag back in the EXACT SAME location when you return home.** You never want to have to search for the location of your document travel bag. People will return your calls at random times with follow-up questions. Therefore, easy access to your document travel bag is essential at all times. It is best to keep your bag in a workspace area where you will likely be handling the papers (a desk or an office). Very few activities involved in settling an estate can be handled only online. Institutions want to verify that they are working with a person who is authorized to handle the estate. This protects both the institution and its customers.

Be prepared to take notes during every meeting or phone call. Highlight any action item that either you or the other person has agreed to complete. Include the date of the conversation and the name of the person contacted. Make notations in this book as you receive new information or complete tasks.

# Keep copies of everything that you send by US Postal Mail. Copy yourself on every email that you send.

Not only will this help you remember what you have sent but if the recipient fails to get what you sent, you can quickly resend the information. It also makes it easy to jointly discuss any follow-up over the phone.

A file drawer can be useful for storing completed paperwork. The following file folders should get you started: Utilities, Tax Statements, Loans/Leases, Credit Cards, Bank Statements, Brokerage Statements, Insurance, Medical Expenses, Employment, Death Certificates, Funeral. You can then adjust as you go.

# INCOME

# DECEASED'S INCOME AT THE TIME OF DEATH

Determine the deceased's income sources that existed at the time of death, then notify the companies or institutions of the death. There may be multiple accounts for each type of income source. If there are minor children or special needs dependents, also determine survivor benefits, including payment terms (amount and timing).

Some payments will stop immediately upon notifying the institution of the death (e.g., Social Security), while others may continue for a while (rental income). Start by notifying those that will immediately stop upon notification of deceased's passing. This will save you the time and hassle of working with those organizations to return any overpaid funds. Your legal counsel can help you with identifying those.

| Type | Institution | Account Number | Contact Person | Contact Information | Current Amount | Future Amount |
|------|-------------|----------------|----------------|---------------------|----------------|---------------|
| Salary | | | | | | |
| Pension | | | | | | |
| Social Security | | | | | | |
| Veterans Affairs | | | | | | |
| Alimony | | | | | | |
| Stocks, bonds & mutual funds | | | | | | |
| Annuity | | | | | | |
| Life insurance | | | | | | |
| 401 K | | | | | | |

| Type | Institution | Account Number | Contact Person | Contact Information | Current Amount | Future Amount |
|---|---|---|---|---|---|---|
| 403 B | | | | | | |
| Traditional IRA | | | | | | |
| Roth IRA | | | | | | |
| SEP | | | | | | |
| SIMPLE | | | | | | |
| Rental income | | | | | | |
| Royalty fees | | | | | | |
| TOTAL MONTHLY INCOME | | | | | | |

# TYPICAL TOPICS TO ASK DECEASED'S EMPLOYER'S HUMAN RESOURCE (HR) DEPARTMENT

When contacting the deceased's employer, you want to discuss more than just stopping the paycheck or pension check. So, I have provided some additional areas to explore with any employer's HR department. Not all these items will apply in every situation. Use this list to get the conversation going with HR to make sure that you obtain all the benefits the estate is entitled to. After you have asked everything that you believe is relevant to your situation, please then ask, **"Are there any other payments or benefits that I didn't ask about that I should have for my situation?"** They are the experts at handling these situations. Let them guide you through the process.

- Accrued regular pay

- Accrued vacation or sick time pay

- Pension and profit-sharing plans

- Stock options

- Life insurance

- Qualified retirement account funds

- Flexible spending and HSA accounts

- Unreimbursed business or medical expenses, including final medical bills

- COBRA insurance options for minor children or special needs dependents

- Other benefits for minor children or special needs dependents

- Picking up deceased's personal effects from office

- Returning company's keys, badges, etc. to company

Be sure to also contact any former employers to see if there are any death benefits or Qualified Retirement Funds.

# EMPLOYER AND GOVERNMENT SURVIVOR INCOME AND BENEFITS

Use this chart to summarize the information for both government and employer benefits.

| Benefit | Amount | Start Date | Payout Amount | Payout Frequency | End Date |
|---------|--------|------------|---------------|------------------|----------|
|         |        |            |               |                  |          |
|         |        |            |               |                  |          |
|         |        |            |               |                  |          |
|         |        |            |               |                  |          |
|         |        |            |               |                  |          |
|         |        |            |               |                  |          |
|         |        |            |               |                  |          |

# REVISED INCOME

If there are no minor children or special needs dependents, there will be no income once the estate is settled. There may be income from rental property, or a business until those assets are disposed of. This table can be used to remind you of those remaining income sources that you have to address. Follow any provisions made by the decedent for handling those funds. Any ongoing income for individuals with special needs or minor children will have to be properly deposited into correct accounts.

| Source | Monthly Amount | Payment Frequency | Date Paid | Comments |
|---|---|---|---|---|
|  |  |  |  |  |
|  |  |  |  |  |
|  |  |  |  |  |
|  |  |  |  |  |
|  |  |  |  |  |
|  |  |  |  |  |
|  |  |  |  |  |
|  |  |  |  |  |
|  |  |  |  |  |
| TOTAL: |  |  |  |  |

# ASSETS

# FINANCIAL ASSETS

**Bank Accounts, Investment Accounts, Retirement Accounts, Insurance Policies, and Annuities**

The first part of this section focuses on the deceased's financial assets and the allocation of those assets to either paying creditors or transferring to the named beneficiaries. Reminder: These funds will be available to you only after proper notification of the deceased's death to the institution by you the executor or trustee and verification that you are legally allowed to handle these funds.

You will need to have previously established a bank account in the name of the deceased's estate or a trust account with you as the trustee. Then the bank can correctly write the name of the account on the cashier's check as each account is closed out and you can pay creditors. Make sure all bills are paid in priority order before distributing funds to those who inherit.

Many times, accounts may have transfer-on-death provisions, or beneficiaries may be named on some accounts. If the documentation of the financial account itself has one stipulation for the beneficiary and the will or trust states something different, usually there are laws in place indicating which takes precedent. Work with your legal representative on this.

To make it easier for you to monitor your progress in settling the various accounts, separate tables have been created for

- Bank accounts
- Brokerage accounts
- Retirement accounts
- Insurance policies and annuities

The bank and brokerage accounts will also likely be the source of funds to pay any of the estate's outstanding bills. That requires that those funds are in an account that you have the legal authority to use.

# BANK ACCOUNTS

Reminder: If your name is not on the account, the funds will be available only after proper notification to the institution that you are the executor or trustee. You then can transfer these funds to a bank account in the name of the deceased's estate or a trust account with you as the executor or trustee, respectively, as you close out each of the deceased's accounts.

Note if any of these accounts are held jointly with others. Seek guidance from the institution and your legal representative for the process to obtain proceeds on behalf of the estate and to remove the deceased's name from any jointly held account.

| Institution | Account Type & Number | Value | Ownership | Contact Information | Username | Password |
|---|---|---|---|---|---|---|
|  |  |  |  |  |  |  |
|  |  |  |  |  |  |  |
|  |  |  |  |  |  |  |
|  |  |  |  |  |  |  |
|  |  |  |  |  |  |  |
|  |  |  |  |  |  |  |
|  |  |  |  |  |  |  |
|  |  |  |  |  |  |  |
|  |  |  |  |  |  |  |

# INVESTMENT ACCOUNTS

Note if any of these accounts are held jointly with others. Seek guidance from the institution and your legal representative to remove the deceased's name from any jointly held account and the process to obtain proceeds to the estate.

| Institution | Account Type & Number | Value | Ownership | Contact Information | Username | Password |
|---|---|---|---|---|---|---|
|  |  |  |  |  |  |  |
|  |  |  |  |  |  |  |
|  |  |  |  |  |  |  |
|  |  |  |  |  |  |  |
|  |  |  |  |  |  |  |
|  |  |  |  |  |  |  |
|  |  |  |  |  |  |  |
|  |  |  |  |  |  |  |
|  |  |  |  |  |  |  |
|  |  |  |  |  |  |  |

# QUALIFIED RETIREMENT PLANS

These include Traditional and Roth IRAs, 401K, 403B, SEPS, SIMPLES, etc. These accounts will likely be handled through the deceased's employer, brokers, or financial advisors. Because there are tax sheltering consequences to the beneficiary based on how and when the beneficiary receives the funds, you as the Executor should not just immediately cash out and close the account.

Your responsibility is to notify the institution of the death and to make any beneficiaries aware of their inheritance. Check with your legal representation to make sure you handle your responsibilities correctly. Once the funds have been transferred from the decedent's account to the beneficiary, then close the account.

**The beneficiaries will have to establish special named accounts to maintain the tax sheltering benefits of the IRAs**. Encourage the beneficiaries to meet with their advisors to determine how best to transfer these funds to meet their needs.

The beneficiaries of the funds do have a window of time in which to make their determination of how they will receive the funds so be prepared for the transfer to potentially take longer than with closing other accounts.

# DECEASED'S QUALIFIED RETIREMENT ACCOUNTS

| Account | Type | Policy Number | Value | Contact Name | Contact Number | Beneficiaries |
|---------|------|---------------|-------|--------------|----------------|---------------|
|         |      |               |       |              |                |               |
|         |      |               |       |              |                |               |
|         |      |               |       |              |                |               |
|         |      |               |       |              |                |               |
|         |      |               |       |              |                |               |
|         |      |               |       |              |                |               |
|         |      |               |       |              |                |               |

# INSURANCE POLICIES AND ANNUITIES

The deceased's death may have triggered the payout of policies, such as:

- Individual life insurance, group life insurance, employer-based life insurance, accident/medical care insurance, long term care insurance, association-sponsored insurance
- Credit life insurance for credit cards or bank-sponsored insurance, mortgage insurance, union-sponsored insurance, property insurance, travel insurance (See CREDIT LIFE INSURANCE TABLE on page 39).
- Annuities

**Always verify whether there is any part of a prepaid premium that can be returned to the estate.**

| Company | Name on Policy | Policy Number | Death Benefit | Beneficiaries | Payout Terms | Contact Name & Number |
|---|---|---|---|---|---|---|
| | | | | | | |
| | | | | | | |
| | | | | | | |
| | | | | | | |
| | | | | | | |
| | | | | | | |
| | | | | | | |

# NON-FINANCIAL ASSETS

These can include items such as the deceased's homes, cars, boats, RVs, coins, guns, jewelry, collectibles, and miscellaneous household goods that the deceased had. Decide how you will dispose of each of these assets.

| Asset | Current Value | Amount Owed | Owner | How To Dispose Of? |
|---|---|---|---|---|
|  |  |  |  |  |
|  |  |  |  |  |
|  |  |  |  |  |
|  |  |  |  |  |
|  |  |  |  |  |
|  |  |  |  |  |
|  |  |  |  |  |
|  |  |  |  |  |

# SUMMARY OF THE COST BASIS OF ASSETS

There is a term called *step-up in cost basis* that is applied to many of a deceased person's assets (house, stock, bonds, etc). The *cost basis* is the price of an asset for tax purposes. A *step-up in cost basis* is applied to property transferred at death. It is the fair market value of the asset at the time of death, not when it was purchased.

When the *cost basis* is increased, there will be less profit when the item is sold, resulting in fewer taxes being paid. Therefore, it is important to know what those *cost basis* values are and to document how those values were determined. Summarize those items in the following tables on the next two pages.

Check with your accountant to get the most up-to-date list of items for which you will need to determine the *stepped-up cost basis*. The asset inventory cost basis is divided into the next two tables – financial and non-financial assets.

This cost basis information will be needed to calculate income to beneficiaries as they file their income tax returns. The IRS 1041 form is used for determining the reportable income, if any, for those who are inheriting from the estate. Beneficiaries must receive a 1041 K-1 with this information. You have to make sure a Form 1041 K-1 is sent to all the beneficiaries annually until the estate is closed out. An accountant can complete the 1041 paperwork, including K-1 forms for each beneficiary.

There may also be an estate tax to be paid on larger estates. Your accountant can give you further details on these taxes for both state and federal levels. If your accountant indicates that the estate needs to complete IRS Form 706 (United States Estate (and Generation-Skipping Transfer) Tax Return), there is a book I previously wrote – *What's My Potential Exposure to Estate Taxes?* – which contains tables you can use to capture and summarize the information for your accountant.

# ASSET INVENTORY WITH COST BASIS – PART 1: FINANCIAL ASSETS

| Asset | Institution | Account Number | Current Value | Cost Basis & How Determined | Beneficiaries |
|---|---|---|---|---|---|
| | | | | | |
| | | | | | |
| | | | | | |
| | | | | | |
| | | | | | |
| | | | | | |
| | | | | | |
| | | | | | |
| | | | | | |
| | | | | | |
| | | | | | |

# ASSET INVENTORY WITH COST BASIS – PART 2: NON-FINANCIAL ASSETS

| Asset | Current Value | Cost Basis & How Determined | Beneficiaries |
|-------|---------------|----------------------------|---------------|
|       |               |                            |               |
|       |               |                            |               |
|       |               |                            |               |
|       |               |                            |               |
|       |               |                            |               |
|       |               |                            |               |
|       |               |                            |               |
|       |               |                            |               |

# LIABILITIES

This includes home mortgages, equity lines of credit, student loans, and notes payable.

List all the liabilities that the deceased had on page 38. If a person dies with a balance owed on some debts, a credit life insurance policy on that account may activate, paying part or all of the balance owed at the time of the deceased's death. These policies are sometimes found on credit cards, mortgages, travel insurance, auto insurance, homeowner insurance, or federal student loans. As you contact the institutions where the deceased had the debts, ask how much, if any, debt forgiveness there is. Note the amounts in the table on page 39. You can also check your copy of the contract. These policies may help reduce the amount the estate needs to pay off the debt.

# MORTGAGES, LOANS, AND NOTES

**(Including home mortgages, equity lines of credit, student loans, and notes payable)**

Before contacting the institutions, read page 37 about credit life insurance policies and any other debt forgiveness. The remaining debts are to be paid in priority payment order when assets are insufficient to cover all the deceased's debts. Please consult your legal help for guidance.

| Mortgages, Loans, & Notes | Person/Company Being Paid | Contact Info | Payment Terms | Remaining Balance | Amount in Arrears |
|---|---|---|---|---|---|
|  |  |  |  |  |  |
|  |  |  |  |  |  |
|  |  |  |  |  |  |
|  |  |  |  |  |  |
|  |  |  |  |  |  |
|  |  |  |  |  |  |
|  |  |  |  |  |  |
|  |  |  |  |  |  |
| **TOTAL UNPAID BALANCES** |  |  |  |  |  |

# ENACTING CREDIT LIFE INSURANCE POLICIES

List the results of any credit life insurance policy debt forgiveness.

| Institution | Contract Number | Contact Person | Phone Number | Amount Owed | Amount Forgiven |
|---|---|---|---|---|---|
|  |  |  |  |  |  |
|  |  |  |  |  |  |
|  |  |  |  |  |  |
|  |  |  |  |  |  |
|  |  |  |  |  |  |
|  |  |  |  |  |  |
|  |  |  |  |  |  |
|  |  |  |  |  |  |
|  |  |  |  |  |  |
|  |  |  |  |  |  |

# BILLS/EXPENSES

While there are usually regular payments made for loans and mortgages, they aren't the only expenses that a person has.

So, list all the remaining bills that the deceased had in the tables on the next two pages. Find both the bills that are paid electronically and those for which checks are written. The last monthly checking account or credit card statements will be a good source, but also remember that there are bills that are paid only quarterly or annually.

Indicate what company is being paid, how much, how often, and through which account. Then either immediately cancel those services or give the company the new account information for autopay, until such time as you can cancel the service.

All creditors need to be notified of any individual's death (local legal paper). Work with your attorney to make sure that is handled properly.

**There is a priority order in which debts of any estate are to be paid before the distribution of assets to beneficiaries. Please obtain legal advice about this before paying any bills or distributing any funds to those who inherit.**

# CURRENT BILLS HELD IN THE DECEASED'S NAME <u>ONLY</u>

Before you pay any of the deceased's debts, first determine whether there are any credit life insurance policies available to pay all or part of these bills, or if the company has a policy on payment of the deceased's final bill. The companies themselves can tell you or you can find it in the original contract. Then list the bills that remain after enacting credit life insurance policies or institution debt forgiveness.

| Institution | Account Number | Service/ Product Paid For | Paid Through Account Name & Number | Amount Due | Date Due |
|---|---|---|---|---|---|
| | | | | | |
| | | | | | |
| | | | | | |
| | | | | | |
| | | | | | |
| | | | | | |
| | | | | | |
| | | | | | |
| | | | | | |
| | | | | | |
| | | | | | |

| Institution | Account Number | Service/ Product Paid For | Paid Through Account Name & Number | Amount Due | Date Due |
|---|---|---|---|---|---|
| | | | | | |
| | | | | | |
| | | | | | |
| | | | | | |
| | | | | | |

# CURRENT BILLS HELD JOINTLY WITH OTHERS

Notify all these accounts of the decedent's death and resolve any ongoing obligations of the estate to pay these bills. Work with the institution and your legal representative to correctly remove the estate from the account and any future responsibility/liability.

| Institution | Account Number | Service/ Product Paid For | Paid Through Account Name & Number | Own With | Amount Due | Date Due |
|---|---|---|---|---|---|---|
|  |  |  |  |  |  |  |
|  |  |  |  |  |  |  |
|  |  |  |  |  |  |  |
|  |  |  |  |  |  |  |
|  |  |  |  |  |  |  |
|  |  |  |  |  |  |  |
|  |  |  |  |  |  |  |
|  |  |  |  |  |  |  |
|  |  |  |  |  |  |  |

# BILLS TO CANCEL IMMEDIATELY

In the tables below, list those bills that you can cancel immediately (typically deceased's gym membership, recreational activity memberships, social memberships, toll collections, print & online subscriptions, charitable organizations, periodicals, mobile devices, and airline mileage accounts).

**You might be able to get a refund of any unused portion of a prepaid fee, so don't forget to ask for that when you are cancelling the service.**

| Company Paid | Product / Service | Date Due | Paid Through Account | Amount | Phone # or Website address | Date Cancelled |
|---|---|---|---|---|---|---|
|  |  |  |  |  |  |  |
|  |  |  |  |  |  |  |
|  |  |  |  |  |  |  |
|  |  |  |  |  |  |  |
|  |  |  |  |  |  |  |
|  |  |  |  |  |  |  |
|  |  |  |  |  |  |  |
|  |  |  |  |  |  |  |
|  |  |  |  |  |  |  |
|  |  |  |  |  |  |  |

# BILLS TO CONTINUE PAYING TEMPORARILY

In the table below, list those bills that you intend to keep temporarily and for how long.  Identify which account you will use to pay the bill.  Then notify the creditor of the new account for making payments.

| Company Being Paid | Old Amount | Paid Through Account | Company Contact | Date 1st Reduced Bill | New Amount | When to Cancel |
|---|---|---|---|---|---|---|
| | | | | | | |
| | | | | | | |
| | | | | | | |
| | | | | | | |
| | | | | | | |
| | | | | | | |
| | | | | | | |

# ONLINE ACCOUNTS

# ONLINE ACCOUNTS

Many wills and trusts now give executors and trustees the authority to handle the disposition of these accounts. Unsubscribe/cancel your deceased's personal accounts. Always check with your lawyer before cancelling any business accounts. The deceased's password list can be an excellent source of which accounts need to be addressed. Some accounts will stop access the minute you notify them of the deceased's death.

| Account Name | Username | Password | Keep or Cancel? | Date Account Cancelled/Transferred |
|---|---|---|---|---|
|  |  |  |  |  |
|  |  |  |  |  |
|  |  |  |  |  |
|  |  |  |  |  |
|  |  |  |  |  |
|  |  |  |  |  |
|  |  |  |  |  |
|  |  |  |  |  |

| Account Name | Username | Password | Keep or Cancel? | Date Account Cancelled/Transferred |
|---|---|---|---|---|
| | | | | |
| | | | | |
| | | | | |
| | | | | |
| | | | | |
| | | | | |
| | | | | |
| | | | | |
| | | | | |
| | | | | |

# RECOMMENDED READING

Byrne, Anna E. *A Widow's Guide: Your Legal and Financial Guide to Surviving the First Year*. United States. North Charleston, SC: Flower Press Publishing, CreateSpace Independent Publishing Platform, 2016. Print

Colgan, Mark R. *Details After Death: Navigating the Logistics After a Loved One Dies*. Pittsford, NY: Plan Your Legacy, 2017. Print.

Hanks, Liza W., and Carol Zolla. *The Trustee's Legal Companion*. Berkeley, CA: Nolo, 2019. Print.

Hoffman, David G. *The Essential Executor's Handbook*. Wayne, NJ: Career Press, 2016. Print.

Houck, Maurcia D. *Living Life After Divorce & Widowhood, Financial Planning, Skills, and Strategies for When the Unthinkable Happens*. Ocala, Fla: Atlantic Pub. Group, 2010. Print.

Munro, Margaret A., and Kathryn A. Murphy. *Estate & Trust Administration*. Hoboken, NJ: For Dummies, a Wiley Brand John Wiley & Sons, Inc, 2019. Print

Phillips, Shane. *First Steps: A Comprehensive Guide to Financial Matters After a Death*. Castle Rock, Colorado: First Step Solutions, LLC, 2013. Print.

Randolph, Mary. *The Executor's Guide: Settling a Loved One's Estate or Trust*. Berkeley, California: Nolo, 2018. Print

Slott, Ed. *The New Retirement Savings Timebomb*. Penguin Books, 2021. Print

# Other Financial Workbooks by Teresa

| Situation | Solution | QR Code and URL to Amazon Book Page |
|---|---|---|
| Widow or widower settling their deceased spouse's estate | *Now What Do I Do? Settling Your Spouse's Estate – Organizing and Simplifying the Process* | https://qrs.ly/mxe03gh |
| Summary of financial and other key information of a married couple (with or without dependent children) | *Our Money Summary – Summary of Family's Finances* | https://qrs.ly/7de03h8 |
| Summary of financial and other key information for an unmarried adult (including recent graduate, widow, divorced, and with or without children) | *My Money Summary – Summary of My Personal Finances* | https://qrs.ly/o6e03ic |
| Assessing how much estate taxes an estate will be required to pay after death | *What's My Potential Exposure To Estate Taxes? Summarizing Data Your Accountant Needs to Estimate Your Estate Taxes* | https://qrs.ly/3qe03ho |
| Outlining your income, expenses, and savings now & in future, so your financial planner can estimate if you will have enough money for your retirement | *Estimating Your Money Gap – Providing for Retirement* | https://qrs.ly/mbe03gu |
| Summarizing key personal and business information for a single, solo business owner, in case of emergency | *Business and Personal Information Summary - for the Single Small Business Owner* | https://qrs.ly/bge03i7 |

**Your Opinion Is Important**

It will help me improve this book and help other readers know what to expect.

If you have an Amazon account, you can scan the QR code below or use the URL to leave a review. *You may be requested to log in to your Amazon account to complete*

*the review form.*

Let me know what you liked best, what was missing, if there was anything you would leave out, or anything else that's on your mind about the book.

Thanks!

https://qrs.ly/1ce01sx